FOOTBALL LEGENDS

Clive Gifford

Copyright © ticktock Entertainment Ltd 2009

First published in Great Britain in 2009 by ticktock Media Ltd,
The Old Sawmill, 103 Goods Station Road, Tunbridge Wells, Kent, TN1 2DP

project editor and picture researcher: Ruth Owen
ticktock project designer: Simon Fenn

Thank you to Lorraine Petersen and the members of nasen

ISBN 978 1 84696 939 3 pbk

Printed in China

Picture credits (t=top; b=bottom; c=centre; l=left; r=right):
AFP/Getty Images: OFC, 4, 5, 8-9, 16-17, 18-19, 22-23, 24. Bernard Bisson/Sygma/Corbis: 23 (inset). Marcus
Brandt/epa/Corbis: 26-27. Getty Images: 13, 28, 29, 31. Man Utd via Getty Images: 10, 11. National Geographic/Getty
Images: 12-13. Popperfoto/Getty Images: 6, 7t, 7b, 20-21. Shutterstock: 1, 2-3, 10-11 (background), 13t, 16, 24-25
(background), 25t, 30-31 (background). Bob Thomas/Getty Images: 6 (inset), 14-15, 15t.

CONTENTS

GOAL!

Goals win games! This is why football's greatest legends are famous for scoring or saving goals.

Brazilian player Rogério Ceni has scored more than 80 goals in his career. Most of the goals were from free kicks.

Rogério Ceni

What makes Ceni special?

He's a goalkeeper – the highest scoring ever!

Mia Hamm

Mia Hamm scored an incredible 158 goals for the US women's team. She first played for her country when she was 15 years old.

EARLY LEGENDS

Dixie Dean

In 1925, English football club Everton signed Dixie Dean for just £3,000. He scored 60 goals in the 1927-28 season. This was a record for the English league.

Sir Stanley Matthews

English football star Sir Stanley Matthews began playing in 1932. He retired 33 years later when he was 50. In over 750 matches he did not receive a single yellow card.

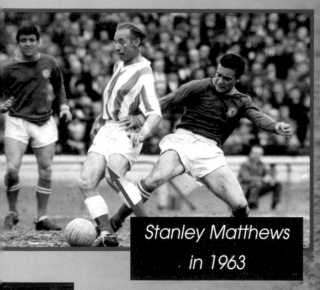

Stanley Matthews in 1963

Ferenc Puskas

In 1953, Ferenc Puskas masterminded Hungary's 6-3 thrashing of England.

Puskas's powerful left foot scored 83 goals in 84 games for Hungary.

Ferenc Puskas, Hungary

Billy Wright, England

Lev Yashin

Russian goalkeeper Lev Yashin saved over 150 penalties in his career.

He was known as "The Black Panther". Yashin retired in 1971.

REAL MADRID

When it comes to legendary football clubs, you do not get bigger than Real Madrid. The team once went 121 home games unbeaten.

In 2008, they won the "La Liga" Spanish League for a record 31st time. They have won the European Cup/Champions League nine times.

(Stats at the end of the 2007/08 season.)

At the start of the 21st century, Real Madrid spent big to create a team of superstars. They were known as the "Galacticos".

Who were the Galacticos ?

- Zinedine Zidane – £45 million

- Luis Figo – £37 million

- Ronaldo – £29 million

- David Beckham – £25 million

MANCHESTER UNITED

Manchester United is England's most famous football club. It was formed as Newton Heath Football Club in 1878.

TEAM STATS

- 17 English League Championships
- 11 FA Cups • 17 FA Charity Shields
- 3 European Cups/Champions League titles

(Stats at the end of the 2007/08 season.)

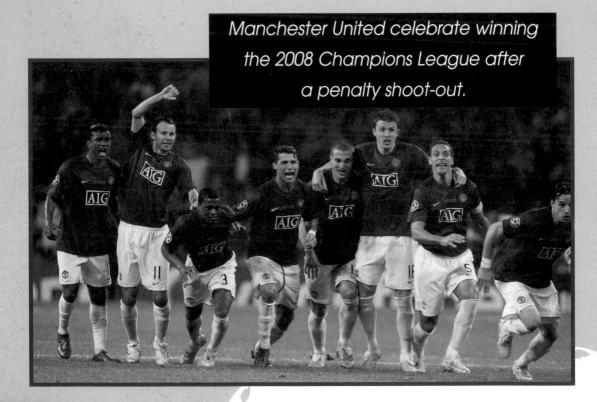

Manchester United celebrate winning the 2008 Champions League after a penalty shoot-out.

Man U's boss, Sir Alex Ferguson has managed the club since 1986. In 1998/99, he led his team to the treble. They won the Premier League, the FA Cup and the Champions League. A record for an English club!

2008 – Ferguson signs Dimitar Berbatov

TRANSFER FEES

First transfer fee: Gilbert Godsmark for £40 in 1900.

Bargain buy: Peter Schmeichel (one of the best goalies ever) for £530,000 in 1991.

Big money buy: Dimitar Berbatov for £30.75 million in 2008.

Strangest fee: Hughie McLenahan for three freezers full of ice cream in 1927.

PELÉ

Pelé was the game's greatest ever player.

Pelé was born into a poor family in Brazil. He shined shoes as a boy to make money.

He became the only player to win three World Cup winners medals.

" How do you spell Pelé? "

G-O-D

A quote from the Sunday Times newspaper

PELÉ STATS

- Scored 1,284 goals
- Played 92 games for Brazil
- Played over 1,000 games for Brazilian club Santos
- Played over 100 games for New York Cosmos

Pelé played for the Brazilian club Santos.
He always wore the number 10 shirt.
Santos retired the shirt when Pelé retired.

1974 – Pelé leaves the pitch after his final game for Santos.

DIEGO MARADONA

Maradona was Argentina's greatest ever player. He scored 34 goals for Argentina.

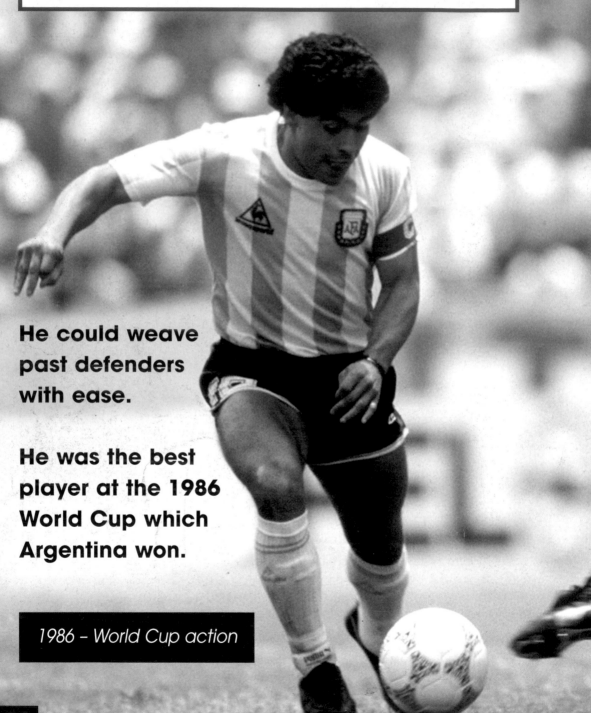

He could weave past defenders with ease.

He was the best player at the 1986 World Cup which Argentina won.

1986 – World Cup action

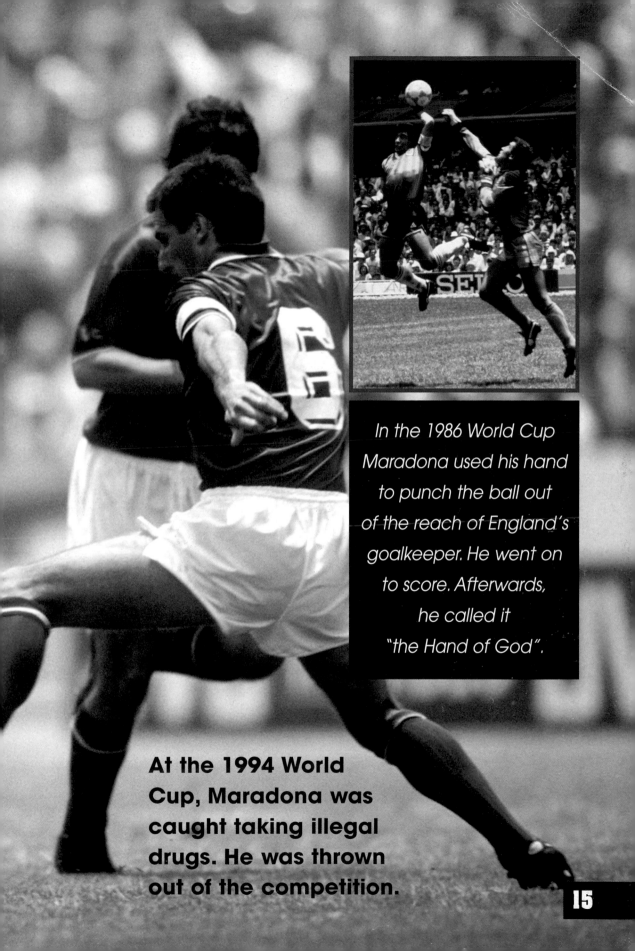

In the 1986 World Cup Maradona used his hand to punch the ball out of the reach of England's goalkeeper. He went on to score. Afterwards, he called it "the Hand of God".

At the 1994 World Cup, Maradona was caught taking illegal drugs. He was thrown out of the competition.

JOHAN CRUYFF

Opponents thought Cruyff was a centre forward. But he would pop up all over the pitch!

Cruyff scored 33 goals for the Dutch national team.

Cruyff was the first player:

- To be crowned "European Footballer of the Year" three times.

- To pass the ball when taking a penalty, receive a pass back and score.

- To have a move named after him. "The Cruyff turn" is a surprise turn that allows a player to shake off an opponent.

1974 – Cruyff at the World Cup

GIANLUIGI BUFFON

In 2000, Lazio smashed the world record fee for a goalkeeper. They bought Angelo Peruzzi for £11.4 million.

Just one year later, Juventus bought Gianluigi Buffon for £32 million!

Most fans think he's worth it.

At the end of the 2007/08 season, Buffon's medals included:

- UEFA Cup winner – 1999
- Italian Serie A League Champion – 2002, 2003
- Italian Super Cup Winner – 1999, 2002, 2003
- Serie A Goalkeeper of the Year – 6 times
- World Cup Winner – 2006

Buffon dives for the ball during training.

BOBBY MOORE

In 1966, Bobby Moore lifted the World Cup. Moore was a brilliant defender and England's greatest ever captain.

BOBBY MOORE STATS

- Over 600 games for English club West Ham United
- 108 games for England
- Played 90 games as England captain
- Scored 2 goals for England

" He was my friend as well as the greatest defender I ever played against.

Pelé **"**

" My captain, my leader, my right-hand man. He was the spirit and the heartbeat of the team.

England manager,
Sir Alf Ramsey **"**

" There should be a law against him. He knows what's happening 20 minutes before everyone else.

Scotland manager, Jock Stein **"**

ZINEDINE ZIDANE

Zinedine Zidane grew up wanting to be a policeman. Instead, he became the world's most expensive footballer.

Real Madrid paid £45 million pounds for Zidane.

Zidane was "FIFA World Player of the Year" three times. He won the World Cup in 1998 with France and the European Championship in 2000.

Zidane lost it in the 2006 World Cup Final. He headbutted Italy's Marco Materazzi and was sent off in his last ever competitive game.

He was still voted the best player of the tournament.

What did Zidane have?
- Touch • Vision • A great pass
- A powerful shot

1998 – Zidane scores in the
World Cup final against Brazil.

Zidane makes a good
pass under pressure.

PAOLO MALDINI

Paolo Maldini is one of the greatest defenders of all time.

Maldini played his first game for AC Milan in 1985.
He still plays for the same club today!
His father, Cesare, also played for AC Milan.

Maldini's record includes:

- 2007 – the oldest player to score in a Champions League final. He was 38 years old.

- 1994 – The first defender to win *World Soccer* magazine's "World Player of the Year" award.

The English Premier League is now the place to be. However, Maldini refused to leave Milan for another club.

" I have great respect for the Premier League, but why leave Milan? I've got everything I want here. Milan is my family. "

Paolo Maldini

FEMALE LEGENDS

Women's football has created its own legends.

Marta Vieira da Silva
Country: Brazil
Club: Umea IK

- Top scorer at 2007 World Cup with 7 goals.
- Scored 47 goals in just 44 games for Brazil.

Many football fans say da Silva is the best women's player in the world.

Birgit Prinz
Country: Germany
Club: FFC Frankfurt

- Won 4 UEFA Women's European Championships.
- Won 2 World Cups.
- Has scored over 120 goals for Germany.

In 2003, Prinz was offered a transfer to the men's Italian Serie A club, Perugia.

DAVID BECKHAM

David Beckham is the only England player to score in three World Cups.

He is one of a small band of players with over 100 England caps.

Beckham is famous for his swerving crosses and free kicks.

DAVID BECKHAM STATS

- 61 goals for Manchester United
- Only player to captain England while playing for a US club (LA Galaxy)
- Only England player to be sent off twice

In August 2008, Beckham was voted "Teen Choice Male Athlete" in the USA. He beat US superstars from basketball and baseball.

Three weeks later, Beckham represented the UK at the Closing Ceremony of the Beijing Olympics.

Need to know words

cap An appearance in the full national football team.

centre forward An attacker who plays closest to the other team's goal.

Champions League
See European Cup.

defender A player whose main role is to stop the other side from scoring goals.

European Cup
The competition that became the Champions League in the early 1990s. Top league teams from each European country compete for the cup every year.

European Championship
A competition between the best national teams in Europe. The competition takes place every four years.

FA Charity Shield A match played at the start of the English league season. It is usually played between last season's FA Cup winner and the League winners.

FA Cup A very popular knockout competition for clubs in England and Wales.

Italian Super Cup A cup competition for the best clubs in Italy.

league A group of teams who compete to win a championship. Each team plays all the others in the league at least once.

Premier League The top level of English club football.

Serie A The top football league in Italy.

UEFA Cup A cup competition for European clubs who finish well in their country's league, but not high enough to enter the Champions League.

vision (in soccer) The ability to spot passes and moves that other players are slow to see.

ALL-TIME GREATS

- In 1967, two armies which were at war in Nigeria, stopped fighting for 48 hours. Why? To watch Pelé take part in a friendly match!

- Diego Maradona hosted his own television chat show in Argentina. It was called *The Night Of The Number 10*. His guests included Pelé, Zidane and Ronaldo.

- In 2008, English club West Ham United retired the number 6 shirt in honour of Bobby Moore.

2008 – Pelé and David Beckham at a football charity event.

FOOTBALL ONLINE

Websites

http://www.ifhof.com/hof/halloffame.asp

http://www.planetworldcup.com/LEGENDS/wcstars.html

http://www.cruijff.com/eng/

http://www.davidbeckham.com/

Index